Viewing the Bible Differently
Updated and Enhanced

How does a person's career and personality type influence how they interpret the biblical narratives?

Michael H. Koplitz
Sandra J. Koplitz
Deborah Hill
A. Robert Cook

This edition 2024 copyright © by Michael H. Koplitz

Published by Michael H. Koplitz

Table of Contents

Acknowledgements

The Bible becomes more interesting when viewed through different lenses. The Bible is a living document that speaks. The book aims to aid readers in comprehending how people with varied experiences interpret the Bible. We must accept all interpretations of the Bible unless the interpretation is un-biblical. Rabbi Steinsaltz said that every person develops their own Torah. Each of us will canonize the Bible that helps them to hear the LORD speaking to them.

Thank you to Sandra, Deborah, and Robert for their contributions to this work. Each of them has been study partners with me over the years in different capacities. We have all learned more about the ways of the LORD by reading and interpreting the Bible and Zohar together. May the LORD continue to bless our working together.

Forward
(A. Robert Cook)

Let us posit at the beginning that there is no one uniform interpretation of a biblical text that everyone can agree on. Our social location will greatly influence our perception of a biblical text. Social location refers to our gender, race, class and income, our political persuasion, our sexuality, our nationality and how we related to other people in our community and outside of our community.

Our awareness of our social location is often poor due to the way we accept how we see the world individually or within our specific social grouping. When one's awareness and understanding of their social location is low, the tendency to see others through our own world view without bias is very difficult. In order to appreciate how we approach a biblical text, it is important, even urgent, to realize our place with our society and to understand that we cannot easily import a biblical text from 2500 years ago into the 21st century without understanding our own biases.

The objective of this book is to help the reader appreciate their view of life and society and disaggregate their view from the historical setting of a text so as to better understand and interpret that text in a way consistent with the biblical narrative.

Introduction
(Michael H. Koplitz)

One day I was visiting my son at his home. It was a regular visit because it is important to see my grandchildren. When my lovely bride and I were ready to leave, my son handed me a book. He told me I would find it interesting. I asked him if he read the book. He told me he had not read it yet. However, the book was written by Scott Adams of Dilbert fame. Scott Adams has written several books about leadership which I had read in my prior computer engineering career.

I am currently a retired pastor and I do biblical research. Allow me to place my advertisement for that work here. You can find it at http://michaelkoplitz.info._Now, let us return to the story. I have a Doctorate in Christian Leadership, so

He thought I would like the book, and that was kind of him to think about me. Initially, I thought of saying thanks, but no thanks. Instead, I borrowed the book and read it on my first vacation week. I found the book extremely insightful. As I reached the end of the book, I had the idea, perhaps divine, that Scott Adams' approach to what he termed "loserthink" applied to how people view the Bible.

Let us start by understanding that people view the Bible in different ways. How can this be? Isn't the LORD's word clear? It is absolutely not simple. I earned my Ph.D. in Hebraic Studies in Christianity, which taught me how to interpret the Bible like Jesus and his contemporaries. I learned the method and added more to the process over time, and today I call it "Semitic Bible Studies." I learned how the Sage Hillel interpreted the Bible. I added the understanding of the culture of Jesus' day and his languages, Aramaic and Hebrew, to hear the Bible the way people in that day did.

Below, I summarized how I learned early in my ministry education career and how people viewed the Bible differently. I will make general statements, so please work with me. At 37 years old, I started a Master of Divinity program at a place called Lancaster Theological Seminary. This was a UCC based seminary in Lancaster, Pennsylvania. When I was at LTS, 1997 to 2002, it was labeled a liberal seminary. Being that I did not grow up in the Church, I had no clue what that meant. Let me tell you, I came from a non-practicing Jewish household. I married a Christian woman who showed Christ to me, and I became a believer. Then I felt called into Jesus' service. He told me to learn the Gospel in its original form as he preached it. I have been working on that calling since 1997 and it will continue all of my life.

The liberal view of Christianity from LTS was interesting. For example, I was told that I could not use any academic resources that came from Moody Publishing. I asked why. The answer was "They only publish conservative materials, which are always wrong." So, I sat in classes with traditionally oriented young people who had an extremely difficult time with what the LTS teachers were saying. Let me give you an example. The Old Testament professor gave us a three-hour lecture on how the prophets' writings did not predict the coming of the Messiah. She then assigned us a reflection paper on the topic. I wrote my paper regurgitating all the points that the professor made. I got an "A" on the paper.

I was in the LTS library after the papers were returned when a younger student came in looking shocked. I thought he was going to cry. He got an "F" on the paper. Why might you ask? The title of his paper was "The Prophets predicted the coming of the Messiah." The professor circled the word predict and then wrote on the reverse side of his paper why he was 100% wrong. She allowed the young student to rewrite the paper. I advised him to repeat everything she said in the lecture. I even gave him a copy of my notes. Guess what, he got an "A" on his rewrite.

LTS's primary goal was to train people to become pastors. Most of the students came in as traditionalists, or maybe we should use the word conservatives, and they were forced into becoming liberal pastors. The big push in the year 2000 was to use feminine language when referring to God. The liberal idea was that pastors offend people, especially women, when God is referred to as a male. Why? Because there were several women who hated their fathers. Therefore, using the word Father to refer to God was offensive.

Imagine what happened to me when I said I cannot call God "Mother" because I disliked my mother. Unfortunately, this is a true feeling. It was offensive to me to think of God as a "Mother." When I said this in the class, every woman attacked me. How can you hate your mother, they shouted at me? It is easy when your mother is a horrible person. That is not the issue here. That was my relationship with my mother. It was that the liberal push was to use feminine language when referring to God.

One Sunday, I filled in for a friend and gave a sermon where I referred to God using feminine language. After the worship celebration, an 80-year-old woman came up to me to give me a lecture that God is a "Father" and not a "Mother." Liberal seminaries are transforming conservative students into liberals and sending them to conservative churches, creating a major problem. Then the poop hits the fan and both the congregation, and the pastor are at odds. The church suffers, and this practice will probably never change.

Now let us move to my doctorate program. I attended Gordon-Conwell Theological Seminary. Gordon-Conwell is a highly conservative seminary. I saw the theology professor at LTS before I attended Gordon-Conwell. He told me I should rethink going to a conservative seminary. While I was at Gordon-Conwell, I went into the library and asked the head librarian where the John Crosson books were. He looked at me very puzzled. He asked me who John Crosson was. For those reading this book and not knowing Crosson, he is one of the top liberal academics. At Gordon-Conwell, I could not use a liberal author. In addition, I could not use any author who did not back everything they said with solid biblical references.

It was interesting to me that the liberal and the conservative seminaries knew little to nothing about the other side. Go to LTS and ask who Marcus Borg was or any other conservative author. When at Gordon-Conwell ask them about a liberal author. I hope you can see how the two seminaries viewed the Bible and the doctrines of faith in completely different ways. The same words of the Bible gave different interpretations. If I said that the prophets of the Old Testaments did not predict Jesus at Gordon-Conwell, I would have been thrown out. I told you what happened when a student said at LTS that the prophets predicted the coming of the Messiah.

Attending seminaries of different ideologies enabled me to comprehend the intricacies of Biblical understanding. Now to Scott Adams's book "Loserthink." Liberal versus conservative is too broad a brush to understand how people view the Bible. It is a great start. Scott Adams offers the way different minds view the world. Each of the views can tell us about how people of different orientations can view the Scriptures. When I say orientations, I need to clarify this. Scott Adams discussed how people of different careers can get caught in a mental prison. Scott Adams coined the term "Loserthink" to describe the mental prison that people create.

In the next pages, I am going to summarize each career orientation, then will postulate how each might view the Bible. If this was to be an academic only type of book, I would have to do research by talking to several people in each of the different careers. I have asked several contributors from different fields to offer their way of thinking and how they view the

Bible. Several of these views are from the book "Loserthink." I will also restate that this work has some generalizations. It is not possible to describe every way a person thinks or feels.

Let me add another thought to this work. I was a computer engineer for 26 years. I spent over 50 hours a week writing programs, designing systems and troubleshooting computers and networks. This was done 48 weeks (sometimes more) per year. My career gave me filters for the rest of my life. Your career will give you filters. When we read the Bible, these filters will affect how we view the narratives. I will give you a spoiler alert. When I wrote the economist view, I saw a new view of the Judas Iscariot betrayal story. I have never read such a view of Judas' motives. However, when I thought about the narrative from the economist's point of view, it became clear. When you get to that section, it will all make sense.

The different views that will be examined are listed here.

1. Viewing the Bible as an Economist
2. Viewing the Bible as a Social Worker
3. Viewing the Bible as an Historian
4. Viewing the Bible as a Teacher
5. Viewing the Bible as an Entrepreneur
6. Viewing the Bible as a Psychologist
7. Viewing the Bible as an Engineer
8. Viewing the Bible as a Leader
9. Viewing the Bible as a Scientist
10. Viewing the Bible as a Pastor

One last thing before you leave the introduction. Who am I writing this book for? Great question! So far, you should know that a conservative (or called traditionalist) views the Bible differently than a liberal (or called progressivist). I wrote this book with contributors to help the pastor, Sunday school teacher, and the Bible study leader. I was a college instructor back in the 1980s for five years. Even though I taught computer science courses, I found it helpful to know how the students' approached problems and how they sought solutions. The same principle applies to Bible study and even sermons.

For Bible studies, if the leader knows how the participants will react to ideas and thoughts, then these ideas and thoughts can be presented clearly. Also, you may have to present thoughts in more than one way. I studied NLP (neurolinguistics programming) in the late 1980s and learned how to determine if a person was a visual, auditory, or kinesthetic learner. My leadership training courses accentuated the three times rule. I changed that statement to: "say it with visuals; say it so they hear it, say it with feelings and emotions." Then every person in the group will understand what you are saying.

Pastors, I did this in my sermons. I created a visual image. I told them how it might sound. I told them how it made people feel. It worked every time! It may be hard for you to believe, but I never had a Sunday sermon bomb. Some were better than others, but never a bomb.

Now, in a small group setting, think about how much more effective you can be if you understand the point of view of the participants. Combine this with NLP and you will hit a home run every time.

The purpose of this book is learning how a person approaches the Bible which will help you help to the person see what God's word is saying.

When you remove the filters of church history and individual assessments, the original meaning of the Bible becomes clearer. I would add that it is important for you to understand that Semitic people wrote the Bible. Their way of writing differed completely from what we westerners learned. This is another area that I will not expand on here, but you can find it in my commentaries and yes, there is a book I wrote on "Ancient Bible Study Methods." The name of the process today is "Semitic Bible Study Methods." I do not mean this to be an advertisement but a passing on of information. You will also read references to the Semitic way of understanding the Bible in some viewpoints in this book.

I do trust that you now have a good grasp about where the book is going to take you. Being aware of your students is one key to success.

I always had a high attendance rate for my Lay Servant classes when I taught them in my church's district. I know this sounds like boasting and Paul says don't do it. I could get the message across to the attendees. The word spread that I did not put the class to sleep and my classes got good attendance.

I hope you enjoy the articles that comprise this book. God bless and Shalom.

Viewing the Bible as an Economist
(A. Robert Cook & Michael H. Koplitz)

(Like Scott Adams, Robert and I are not economists. However, like Scott, we have experience in dealing with finances. Michael was on the Conference Finance and Administration Committee for four years.

In what ways would an economist begin to approach a biblical text?

An economist is a highly trained person, possessing advanced degrees and internships in large corporations or in government, who studies the relationship between a society's resources and its production or output. Economists study societies ranging from small, local communities to entire nations and even the global economy. The expert opinions and research findings of an economist are used to help shape a wide variety of policies, including interest rates, tax laws, employment programs, international trade agreements, and corporate strategies.

Essentially, one who is a qualified economist uses their knowledge base and analytical skills to understand societal trends, issues, finances and real time problems. They will use their critical skills to penetrate beneath the surface questions to ask what is going on in the study being conducted.

The view of an economist is not just on money, although it is said that money makes the world go around. Those who have money tend to use it to pressure people into doing things their way. In today's stock markets, it is the economist who will seek to predict the stocks that will gain or lose value over time and that is quite important. The economist understands budgeting and how to use their resources in the best manner.

Because of their skill at critical thinking, Economists can usually spot a hoax because money drives human behavior in predictable ways.

An economist will look at trends, analyzing things in a cost compared to benefits approach. Perhaps it is risky to invest in a startup company, but if the company takes off, then one might earn a fortune. Of course, there will be failures along the way. An economist will analyze the situation and seek to make the best decision about what is too risky and what is not.

As with most fields, if you ask two different advisors the same question about an investment, you are likely to get two very different answers. The advisors' view may differ. One may like risk while the other is more of an investment conservative. The economist was taught how to make comparisons between multiple options.

So, economists like money, they understand the use of money, and they know how to make and lose money.

Let us examine three very different biblical texts and approach them the way an economist would begin to use their critical skills to arrive at the meaning of the text. We will look at Genesis 3—the story of the serpent tempting Eve; I Samuel 16 –the story of the prophet Samuel anointing the young David as the future king; and, selections from the Gospel of John pertaining to Judas' betrayal of Jesus.

The economist might look at this story and ponder what the risk benefits were for the serpent. There seem to be few benefits if one only is seeking a monetary benefit. Since money did not exist, there must have been something equal to money for the serpent to get. Can the economists who may read this book see it? I am going to tell you the benefits. The Sages of Israel have said that the serpent was the next in line to become stewards of the world. God's first choice was humanity. The serpent thought that if Adam and Eve disobeyed God by eating the forbidden fruit that God might squash humanity and make the serpent the ruler of the world. It was an enormous risk for the serpent. However, an economist might tell you that the risk of rewards was in favor of the serpent. So, the currency sought after was power.

By tricking Eve into trusting him, the serpent was robbing her of her power of freedom and choice. She gave them up unwittingly. However, Adam freely ceased his power of choice and freedom. What was in it for him to do so? Here, the economist would have to use those hard-earned critical skills to penetrate deeper into the story.

The biblical text does not give a reason for Adam's choice, and that means we can only speculate. What were the benefits Adam would gain by following Eve so willingly into disobedience?

Economically, their world was a commonwealth. Resources were gathered, developed and shared for the benefits of all. If their choice was to shut God out of their lives, their naivete led them down a very wrong path. With so much to lose, why did they make so unwise a choice?

The economist likely would not provide a definitive answer, but an analysis of events and the results. Taking such factors into account, an economist would have to predict that humanity had a short and uncertain future. But another factor emerged, and that was God's response. God provided a redemptive response for the couple in our story, and that changed the course of everything. Although, their tendency towards disobedience seems to have a genetic component that has followed humanity down through history, for human beings exhibit the propensity to take happiness and throw it away with both hands in exchange for suffering. Generally speaking, the purpose is to obtain more wealth.

Next, we come to the story of the prophet Samuel being called of God to anoint David, the eighth son of Jesse and the future king of Israel. What a risk benefit analysis that would make. An economist would want to weigh the actions of Samuel against the possible retaliation by the present King, Saul —an unstable and mercurial ruler who was ill-suited to the role of leadership. The economist would clearly see that Saul would take seriously any threat to his power and position and would react with swift vengeance if he discovered Samuel was anointing a future king from another Israelite family. The risk to Samuel was large, which he understood. There was also a risk to the House of Jesse and not just to his son David. The entire family could be wiped out in a purge.

So, do you think the economist would view this story as Saul wanting to protect his power, position and wealth? I think you get the picture of how an economist might automatically seek to follow the money trails. First, I am not saying that the economist's view of these two stories is in any way incorrect. I want to open the economist's eye to see that many biblical narratives do not focus on just money and, most times, not money at all.

Why did Judas betray Jesus? For the economist, the answer is simple: GREED. Greed is something the economist fully understands because greed equals money. I was told by a friend that when I am researching biblical history, I should look at the money trail. The economist would be excellent at doing this. In the Judas story, the church tradition became that Judas was just a greedy man.

Let me give you a couple more examples, then I will discuss how to help the economist see past the money block. What about the incident in the Garden of Eden? The crafty serpent tricked Eve into eating from the forbidden tree. I am sure there are readers who say that it was Satan who tricked her. That is an add on to the story by Bishop Augustine when he developed his original sin doctrine. Since this is not a deep theological book, take my word for it. Or you could get my book on the debunking of original sin. Let's continue with the story.

Mike is a father of three children, 33 months apart in age. When mom went to the grocery store, and I watched the three kids, I had a standing rule. Everyone was guilty and everyone suffered the same fate. I wanted quiet and to get it, I put everyone in their own rooms with the doors closed. Since it was the mid-1980s to mid-1990s, there were no TVs in the kids' rooms. They would have to find their own entertainment. I did not care who was right or wrong.

I did not care who hit who. ALL GUILTY! Fair? Today I will say "No." However, then I got quiet. The person who started the fighting must have thought that a victory was about to occur and there would be some benefit to it. Eventually, they understood how dad handled justice. There was a risk reward to whomever started the confusion.

In the Garden scene, the economist is right in thinking that the serpent did a risk benefit analysis and determined that the reward was worth the risk. The reward would not have been s money and wealth. Instead of the serpent getting all the beauty of God's creation, the humans got it. To the serpent God's creation was valuable. That was easy.

There is the story of David, who was anointed King of Israel by Samuel, the prophet of God. What a risk benefit analysis that would make. An economist would weigh the actions of Samuel versus what David went through. King Saul was not pleased that his sons would not be taking the thrown after him. Saul went after David and tried to kill him. Did I forget to mention that David saved Israel, while Saul was King, when he defeated Goliath? Let us not forget that David was married to one of Saul's daughters. I have heard about father-in-law disagreements, but luckily, most don't end up with a death contract. The economist would see that if Saul was no longer King, he would lose a fortune. The ex-King cannot collect taxes from the people. So, the economist would view this story as Saul wanting to protect his portfolio.

I think you get the picture of how an economist will automatically seek the money trails. So, let's see how we can force the economist to view the Judas and David story from a unique vantage point. First, I am not saying that the economist's view of these two stories is in any way incorrect. I want to open the economist's eye to see that many biblical narratives do

not focus on just money and, most times, not money at all.

The David and Saul story will be seen by an economist as a money story. Saul had the money, and he refused to give it up. I am sure that was a big factor. The theological position is that God wanted Saul out because he visited a fortune teller before entering a battle. Why is this a big deal? First, because Samuel the prophet told Saul that he had to wait until he returned to start the battle. The second is that the Torah does not like fortune tellers. God removed Saul because he disobeyed God's prophet and the Torah. It was not a money issue.

Yes, David became rich once King. But it was not wealth that drove David at the beginning. It was obeying God. Read the Davidic Psalms to get an actual picture of how David felt when Saul's army was chasing him in the countryside. It is enlightening. So, when I am working with an economist, I am happy to enhance the money parts of the story because they will like that part. I add the benefits-rewards if applicable. Then I try to open the economist's eyes to seeing that God is behind the stories. God is not physical, but spiritual. God does not care about money. He cares about souls.

Let us return to the 30 pieces of silver that Judas received to betray Jesus. The silver was thirty silver coins called denarii. When the economist learns what a denarius was worth, the view of a money trail should change. So, what was a denarius worth? That was a wage given to a laborer in a field for a day's work, usually 10 to 12 hours. Judas received one month of salary to betray his rabbi, his teacher, and his friend. Was it worth a month's salary to betray Jesus? Even the economist should agree with this understanding that something else was afoot. The thirty pieces of silver correspond to an Old Testament story. Therefore, it is an allegory that Judas received thirty pieces of silver. There had to be a bigger motive. Here's the cool economic rub.

Judas Iscariot was a Zealot. The Zealots wanted to rid Judea from Roman rule since the Romans invaded in 68 BCE. Messianic tradition said that the Messiah would start the armed revolt, win the war, and become the new King of Judea. But Jesus did not do it. Judas knew that Jesus' time was short. So, Judas took matters into his own hands and tried to force Jesus to start the revolt. It was only after Jesus was arrested and stopped Peter from starting an armed revolution, that Judas realized he was following the wrong Messianic tradition. Judas then hung himself.

Wait a minute, I said that Judas had an alternative which led to money. It was not the thirty pieces of silver he cared about. Imagine the wealth the Zealots would have had if they defeated the Romans. The

Zealots would have taken over the Temple and the government. Oh yeah, TAXES. The Zealots would have then taxed the people and became rich. So, there was an economic backdrop to the story. I hope any economists reading this can see why Judas might have been greedy, but not for a mere thirty silver denarius. Call Judas' greedy because of the taxes the Zealots could have garnished from the people of Judea! I never viewed this story in this manner. This thought dawned on me when examining the Judas story as an economist.

Viewing the Bible as a Social Worker
(Deborah Hill LCSW)

I would be remiss to suggest that all Judeo-Christian social workers perceive the scriptures similarly. People come to the profession of social work from various backgrounds and experiences that shape the individual's views on scripture prior to their launching into the profession.

A social worker can be found performing mental health, drug, and alcohol services, helping the homeless, working to protect and save abused children and adults, in hospitals and emergency rooms, hospice care, police and fire departments, immigration preparation, insurance companies, prisons, and working in government to change laws that disenfranchise the population of people they serve. I'm sure I have missed many other environments where a person could find themselves in contact with a social worker.

According to the National Association of Social Work, the job of a social worker is to restore and enhance the functioning of individuals (micro), families and groups (mezzo) and communities (macro). We subscribe to a regimented code of ethics consisting of the highest standard of service, social justice, dignity and worth of a person, importance of human relationships, integrity, and competence.

According to the University at Buffalo School of Social Work, social workers have the following attributes:

Good Communicator

Empathetic

Active Listener

Critical Thinking

Problem Solving

Culturally Aware

Objective

Emotionally Intelligent

Organized

Ethics Oriented

Advocacy

Patience

Flexibility

Compassionate

Resilient

When looking at how a social worker views scripture I need to use a subset of social work, the mental health practitioner. I chose this because although now retired, I spent most of my career as a clinical social worker, a mental health practitioner. Again, this in no way speaks to the entire consortium of mental health social workers.

As a clinical social worker, I was taught life is a journey filled with insurmountable perceptions, actions, consequences, and decisions based on a person's inner world vs their outer world. It is an attempt to get their perceived needs met by behaving in ways to bring the inner and outer world more in balance. A person can control themselves and only has a limited ability to control others.

In my clinical practice, I was confronted with people from all walks of life and religions. I got to hear firsthand and see how a person's views on scripture or other spiritual writings made a difference in healing. I got bombarded with questions like, why did a higher power allow this to happen? In clinical social work, you do not push your faith/spiritual journey on clients.

Speaking from my experience, as a social worker exploring scriptures, I do not take the stories literally. I take them as being the product of someone's environment written thousands of years ago. These writers, often not the originators of the story but a repetition of information passed down verbally through the ages. These writers had very important messages and history they were trying to relay as seen through their perceptions. I often find it helpful to indulge in theories and others' attempts at interpreting scripture. I have a journal with what I call, My Lessons Learned Along My Journey. Currently, I have two hundred and fifty-seven entries. Yes, I do go back and reread them. Many are comments from prominent people through time as they explored the scripture based on their culture, through their perceptions. In viewing different perspectives, I gain awareness of the depth of scripture.

In discussing scripture with others, I listen and ask questions to help me understand how that scripture as seen through their perspective. I take those answers and wrap them around my own perspectives. Then comment with my understanding of that scripture that hopefully does not judge. I feel strongly that each of us has our own journey and truth. My hope is to help along their journey while enlightening my own in building my relationship with God.

To better show how I view scriptures, a question was posed to me. In the book of Hosea, why did Hosea marry a prostitute? Since this is not a discussion with others, I will show the steps I took in analyzing the section noted as Hosea 1:2.

> When the LORD first spoke to Hosea, the LORD said to Hosea, "Go, get yourself [a]a wife of whoredom and children of whoredom; for the land will stray from following the LORD."
> Hosea 1:2

I must state in pre-internet times to find this answer, I'd pray for guidance. Then I would use my various copies of the Bible, pick the pastor or priest's brain, talk with others, and try to find books in libraries, religious (affiliated with a church or other religious institution) and secular. If I could not find an answer that I felt in my heart to be truth, I would then start looking at other religious teachings to see if I could find similarities to give me a broader insight into my faith. As I believe you can find God in all cultures.

In finding the answer concerning the marriage of Hosea and Gomer, first I prayed for guidance. I read the introduction to Hosea and then the book. It would be easy to say, Hosea married a prostitute because God told him to do so. However, more questions arise for me because the notion that God told Hosea to marry a prostitute, and not for her redemption, and naming his children after God's feelings, did not sit right with me. I believe the marriage is probably a metaphor.

My question was suddenly not why did Hosea marry a prostitute, but two other questions; is she really a prostitute and why would God tell him to marry her and not simply use Hosea's prophecy to discuss the relationship between Israel and God?

I have at my disposal different Bibles. I like to cross reference them to see the various translations. For example: I start by looking at the word used to describe the wife, Gomer.

a. In the Amplified Bible, God tells Hosea to marry a HARLOT.

i. "a woman who gives sex to men for money." The Easy English Bible

b. In the Good News Bible, God tells Hosea to marry, but know his wife will be unfaithful.

i. Quite different from a prostitute.

c. In the King James Bible, they call her a woman of WHOREDOM.

i. "a consecrated woman, (Perhaps priestess) devoted to prostitution in honor of some heathen idol." McClintock and Strong Biblical Cyclopedia.

d. In the Catholic Bible, again they call her a woman of WHOREDOM.

e. According to Chabad.org, the Jewish text calls her a HARLOT.

I stop here and decide Gomer, the wife, was a woman involved in providing sex for money or as a part of a cult practice. Or was she? Is the word harlot/whore a metaphor for something else? I research it.

Reading from the writing of Elder Joseph, the Hesychast of Vatopaidi, Greek Orthodox Church (pempotousia.com) by Theodore Rokas, entitled <u>The Prophet Hosea and his Allegorical Marriage</u>.

1. According to Theodoritos Kyrou, "idolatry is what is meant by harlotry." And that "God's punishment and love of Israel is symbolized allegorically … by the marital relations of the prophet with the adulteress…"

2. "the revelation and relationship was reconstructed by Hosea as the relationship between the spouses in married life."

I believe this information to be most likely true, however, it is only one resource. I keep researching. Can I find any reference to back up my thoughts on metaphor other than Theodoritos Kyrou? I start with Wikipedia to find references and move on to other sources.

1. Ehud Ben Zvi, a historian of ancient Israel, talks of the socio-historical context of the story. He has authored an article entitled, "Observations on the marital metaphor of YHWH and Israel in its ancient Israelite contexts; general considerations and particular images in Hosea 1.2." <u>Journal for the study of the Old Testament 28, no. 3:363-84</u>

2. Michael D. Coogan, Biblical scholar states that, "God's disappointment towards Israel is therefore expressed through the broken marriage covenant made between husband and wife." <u>A brief Introduction to the Old Testament: The Hebrew Bible in its Context.</u> This reminds me of the Good News Bible stating God told Hosea to marry and she would stray from the marriage.

As I continue to read, I find several ways theologians and scholars have explored the marriage of Hosea and Gomer. According to Dr. Claude Mariottini, Professor of Old Testament. These range from:

1. E. W. Hengstenberg, German Lutheran theologian, and scholar, believes the marriage is a vision or dream.
2. John Calvin, French theologian, founder of Calvinism, believed the marriage is a parable.

3. An unmentioned sum of Rabbis believe the marriage is an allegory invented by Hosea.

4. Abraham Herschel, Jewish Theologian, states he believes the marriage is literal.

5. James Newsome and C. Hassel Bullock, Biblical scholars, believe the marriage was real.

In this crude research and my proclivity to not see the Bible literally, I believe Hosea or whomever penned the book created the marriage story to demonstrate more succinctly, the idolatry of Israel before the covenant with God and their return to idolatry (perhaps the adulterous Gomer), and God's forgiveness after punishment and Love despite all. Why did Hosea marry a prostitute? My answer, he did not marry a prostitute. The story is a metaphor.

Viewing the Bible as a Historian
(Michael H. Koplitz)

I have always loved to learn about world history. The history channel is one of my favorite channels. It is interesting to compare history from the victor's side and the loser's side. The winners of wars wrote and maintained history from antiquity. The losing side often got destroyed or spread out by the winners (that is what the Assyrians did when they conquered a nation), resulting in the death of their culture and history. Also, the politics of that day and even modern politics can influence written history.

It is sad to see history being rewritten to express a current political situation. For example, some of what happened during the United States civil war is being rewritten. When statues of Confederate Generals and leaders are being destroyed today, it is a rewrite of history. Part of America's history is that the institution of slavery occurred in the southern states. It was absolutely a dark time for the country and should never have happened. However it happened. The truth in the phrase "history repeats itself" is clear when we erase or intentionally forget parts of history. Future generations should maintain what happened in the south as a part of history. The Generals of the Confederate army served in the US army, and many were heroes of the Mexican war. Our ancestors' past mistakes need to be learned from, and we should remember them.

What is interesting about the US civil war was the reasons for the war. Since this is a book about the Bible, I want to add that it was a religious war. Now you are probably said, "say what?" When I took my religion in America class at seminary, the instructor made that statement. After the gasps, he explained that the south believed that slavery was biblical. Even Paul said to slaves that when they came to know Christ, they needed to stay as slaves. The north believed that slavery was not biblical. Each side prayed before going into battle, asking the LORD to support their cause. Theologians who were in both armies wrote this view. The Methodist Episcopal Church split into the North MEC and the South MEC when the war broke out. It was not until 1939 that the two sides reunited.

Fake news occurs on both sides of a conflict. This creates multiple realities. Let me give you a recent, but now historical example. In 2020, during the Covid pandemic, there was rioting in the streets of several major cities in the United States. If you listened to CNN, they called it the summer of love. I watched a segment on the riots in Seattle. Sorry, according to CNN, they were peaceful protests. Behind the reporter, there were several burning buildings and several cars on fire. That was not a peaceful protest. That was a full riot. Rioters destroyed property and killed people. The viewers of liberal news outlets were told that all was peaceful. If you watched FOX news, you got a different story. They called the situation what it was, a riot.

I was watching a news broadcast with live views of a riot in Philadelphia. The live video showed people running in the streets waving guns and shooting each other. My daughter lived in Philadelphia. I called her, being a concerned father, and asked her if the riots were close to where she lived. She assured me it was a mile away and asked me why I was concerned about the peaceful protests in Philadelphia. I told her I was watching a live video of people shooting each other in the streets. She did not believe me. I asked her to turn on FOX news and watch the live videos. My daughter has liberal views, and that is fine. But even a liberal calls a riot "a riot" when it is happening. The point here is that the people writing history today will have a strong political bias, whether they are conservative or liberal minded. It is clear the two sides of the political isle view history differently.

The area of the world called Israel today was once called Palestine. After 135 CE, the Romans destroyed everything in that area. Back then it was called Judea, Samaria, and Galilee. 135 CE was the second Jewish revolt against the Roman Empire. The Romans destroyed the land. Not only did they destroy the cities and towns, they also destroyed all vegetation. They burned all the trees to the ground. Without the trees and plants, the land turned to sand. Only nomads lived in that area. History says that the people called Palestinians today lived in Trans-Jordan and Jordan. Today there is such conflict over this land.

History shows that the peoples in the Middle East had one thing in common: they hated each other. That is a sad conclusion, however history says so.

History can lead us to viewing the Bible in different ways. I already mentioned the US civil war and that both sides viewed slavery differently using the Bible. People rarely use the books 1 and 2 Chronicles in the church. Biblical historians say that southern kingdom authors wrote the books of Hebrew Scriptures (Old Testament) except for the Chronicals. Northern kingdom authors wrote the Chronicles. Since the Assyrians destroyed the northern kingdom, it is incredible that their writings survived. However, the writings made it to us.

Take a moment and read about King David. The books of Samuel and Kings loved David. Even with all of David's missteps and violations, the people loved David. After all, he created a nation from a group of twelve separate tribes. Judaism today loves King David. King Saul comes across as an idiot. Now turn to the Chronicles. King David is a good guy. However, King Saul was a great king who got screwed. It is a completely different view of history. Since Judea survived, they picked the books of the Bible. It is interesting that the rabbis in 90 CE picked the Chronicles for the Bible. Perhaps it was because they wanted something from the northern kingdom to survive. Ten of the twelve tribes comprised the north, and it would have been sad to let them completely die.

From a historical point of view, it is difficult to accept some of the biblical stories from a literary view. A historian would indicate that it would have been impossible for a kid to kill a giant with a smooth stone. Even if David hit Goliath between the eyes, a lucky shot, it would not have had enough speed on it to break through his skull and destroy his brain. It takes a lot of force to crack a human skull. Therefore, historians would question the story from a practical point of view. The acceptance of such a story would have to be on faith with a lot of doubt.

There are numerous narratives in the Bible that do not seem possible from a historical point of view. Here is where I will come in and tell you a fact about the biblical narratives. Theologians wrote them. The authors were people who viewed everything that happened as being ordained by the LORD. The historian should remember that the authors of the biblical narratives saw all events as part of God's plan. That means that God is involved in every narrative!

There is a story about the sun standing still for three days for Joshua during one of the critical battles in the conquest of Canaan. I wrote a book on this subject and explained culturally how that appeared. The bottom line here is that the sun did not stand still for three days. The historian would agree with that. How can you believe such a story? Ok, first a theologian wrote it. Therefore, God must be involved in the story. Joshua won a battle that he probably should have lost. Most of the conquest of Canaan should not have happened when you consider the history of the area. However, Joshua was a great general and planned his victories well. A cool way to write the story is to use hyperbole. Semitic people love hyperbole. The fish caught might have been 6 inches long, but when the story was retold, it grew to 6 feet. That's very Semitic.

I would explain to the historian that we have to sift out the message of the narratives. The God language and divine interventions have to be interpreted into actual events. Let's stop for a second. I am not saying that there was not a David versus Goliath fight, or that the sun did not stand still. First off, I was not there. I've studied the Bible for 25 years and have learned ancient Israel's culture and biblical authors' writing styles. Semitic authors used metaphors and analogies in their writings. Theologians did the writings, and these factors have to be considered.

The historian must understand that these filters have been applied to the stories. The fundamentalist view of accepting the biblical narratives literally does not work. Martin Luther, who pushed this idea, did not know how Semitic people wrote. Why? The church separated itself from Judaism by 135 CE. The capital moved from Jerusalem to Rome before that date. Those educated in the classical style, the Gentiles, learned to read the Bible literally. I call this the Greek way of learning. Plato's academy originated it and people still use it today. There is nothing wrong with the Greek style of learning and writing. However, this is not the way Semitic people wrote. The historian must remove the filters mentioned and understand the Semitic way of writing. Then the historian can reveal the history of the Bible by understanding the Semitic way of writing after removing the mentioned filters.

The "improbably" stories of the Bible look a lot different when examined as the original authors thought.

Viewing the Bible as a Teacher
(Sandra J. Koplitz)

I am a teacher. I have been one for almost all of my life. At the age of five, I was sitting at the kids' play area of the doctor's office and showing younger ones how to put puzzles together. I knew that teaching something, somewhere, would be my destiny. I have never regretted that path.

I come by this profession naturally. My mother worked in a college bookstore and taught children's Sunday school for many years. My father, through his years, did many things. He was a student pastor while he attended college, then he became a junior high history teacher. He continued his studies and took a position as a school guidance counselor, then a school psychologist and finally a very popular college professor of psychology. He was a great teacher and I learned so much from him about how to engage others in encouraging and interesting ways. Teaching is in my blood!

One of the things my father taught me was how to be a good listener. He also taught me to look for the very best in others. He wanted me to connect with others in an open and compassionate way. This has helped me to be the best teacher I can be as I seek to provide what my students need for success. And more than anything, they need to be heard and encouraged to explore the subject in their own way using their own interests. They need to learn and grow in their own way. They love to have open dialogs about topics and learn from me and each other. It is amazing how they respond to experiencing new thoughts and ideas. We learn from and enlighten each other in so many positive ways. For the last 30 years I have taught every level from pre-school to high school and no matter what the age, the process remains the same. We learn better when we listen to each other and share our insights to help each other grow.

This is how I think we need to approach the study of the Bible. To be good teachers, we also need to be good learners. It is invaluable to be ready to learn new things, adjust our viewpoints with gained knowledge, and incorporate new and different information into our own understandings. Then we look for the lesson in all of it. What use is it to expand our own insights, if we can't find a way to share them with others?

Because I grew up learning about the Bible and its life-changing messages of love and acceptance, I always want to find ways to expand my understanding of the great stories on those pages. Those of us who "grew up in church" learned all of the amazing stories like the Garden of Eden, the life of Moses, the many times

Israel was conquered and survived , and of course the wonderful teachings of Jesus and the travels of his disciples. Yet, there had to be more to the story than just, "God helped little David slay the giant Goliath". As children, we learned the "moral of the story" but we were not ready to understand why he was in that situation, what was the history of the time, or what that event meant to the people of David's time and how it might affect God's people in the future.

Hundreds of these stories in both the Old and the New Testaments lead us to a very basic insight into how God has given life, strength, and hope to those who follow Him. But does it simply stop there? Many people who have attended church for decades are still happy to just hear those comforting old stories again and again.

As a teacher and life-long learner, I want more. God is so vast and infinite, there must be more that He offers to us to learn, understand and apply to our lives. I believe that his richest and most precious gifts come to us as we mature in our understanding of his love and presence in our lives. I never want to stop exploring God's Word and the lessons that other believers can bring to it through their own experiences and points of view.

The personal connections that other followers of God share with us and the many scholars who have studied both the languages and cultures of those ancient times and Biblical heroes, can bring so much depth to our understanding and application of those messages. This allows us to not only be enlightened by a more comprehensive view of what God wants us to absorb and appreciate about His connection to us. We then share the lessons we have learned and the feelings we have about God's exceptional words and apply them to better our lives. There are so many resources for learning more about the original meaning of those events written in our scriptures, but most of us have never heard of them. We have only scratched the surface of understanding what those who wrote it had to tell us about God's ways of caring for the people He created. If we have only been exposed to the modern Christian viewpoints, without considering the insights of the Jewish faith given to us in the Old Testament, then we can miss the rich lessons that allow us to learn and grow in a more spiritual way.

My husband is a Christian Biblical researcher, scholar and writer. With his background in Jewish study, he has found volumes of writings from the ancient sages about the culture of those times and how the people then understood the messages God shared in the same and different ways than they have come to mean today. The language can also be confusing since many words can have several meanings. (As an English example: "The present is a good time to present the present." This shows 3 different meanings for the same word in one sentence.) Our current day understanding of these biblical words could lead us into many different understandings of the message given by the writers. Think of all the interesting things we might learn as we explored each of the possibilities. My husband has been both a great learner, by using the research and background he has gained from these scholars, but also a great teacher in opening up the wonderful words of the Biblical characters in new and different ways. This has made a profound effect on my interest in learning more and more about my faith and its rich history. I want to know so much more, like "When Jacob gave Joseph the coat of may colors, did the specific colors have a significance to the story of his life?" I don't know the answer, but I am guessing that someone has written about it and I can learn from it when I finally find out!

My classroom is beside the room of an English teacher. As her students read a classic novel, she encourages them to find the meanings hidden in the text. Why did the lady wear a green coat? Why is that important? After thinking, evaluating, making connections to other books and exchanging ideas with classmates and the teacher, they find that the lady was "green with envy". The same is true of our sacred scriptures. So much is lost if we just read the Greek or Hebrew words translated into English without reaching to understand the depth of possible knowledge and insights available to us through further study. These Biblical texts are much more important to us than any novel ever written.

Great teachers encourage us to explore this knowledge and learn to incorporate these new thoughts and understandings into our already firm foundations of faith in our ever-present, ever-loving God. Once we are open to accepting that there is much more to learn, the real excitement begins!

Teaching and learning go hand-in hand. As I learn more about what historical and cultural information is available to view the words and actions of Biblical characters through the lens of their own time, I am amazed at the possibility of getting closer to my God. And when that happens, thanks to the discourse with others more educated than I am, it creates an excitement that I want to share with others.

Any teacher will tell you that this sharing is the best part of the work we do. I get to open growing minds to new ideas and knowledge and then encourage the learners to share their ideas and thoughts so that we grow in understand together with God's help. This brings us together as a family of faith. I might say, "Let me learn how you connect to God and His word and let me share my connections with you. Then we both help each other grow in faith. All our lives, physical and spiritual, will be enriched by grace and hope in the Author of Life."

Viewing the Bible as an Entrepreneur
(Michael H. Koplitz)

When one thinks about entrepreneurs, it is usually of a businessperson, someone like Elon Musk who has the gift to build new companies, like Tesla, and to reinvigorate dying companies like Twitter. Business entrepreneurs like to think outside the box. We can also find this spirit in people who are not business entrepreneurs.

Let me introduce myself as an entrepreneur spirit. I have not created a new business or industry. However, I think outside of the box. Through my experiences, I have learned to solve problems in different ways. I love the meaning of Yahoo—you always have other options. When I was in my computer engineering career, I became known as the guy who could make it happen. My last employer was

Warner-Lambert Inc., and the plant was in Lititz, Pennsylvania. Unfortunately, I have to inform you that the company was acquired 20 years ago and split into discrete entities. I recently heard that the Lititz plant was being shut down. The end of an era.

I worked on a time and attendance system for the plant floor. I developed the system and wrote the programming for most of it. The system worked well until its third day. The computer that ran the system became one minute behind the plant's master clock. Oh, the shock! Ok, you may laugh at this, and I am going to tell you why this happened. First, this is not a condemnation of union people. The union created a grievance against the computer that day. The factory people would line up at the time and attendance terminal several minutes before the end of the shift. When the end of shift bell rang, the time and attendance clock said they had one minute left to work. They had to wait that minute to scan out for the day. I found this incredible. One minute really. Oh yes, this problem had to be solved. My boss called in Digital Equipment Company to help solve the problem. The plant used DEC computer equipment. Oh yes, let me also say that this occurred in 1994.

DEC wanted $50,000 to connect the master clock to the server, which controlled the time and attendance clocks. I investigated the situation since I was the project manager and said to the boss, I could do the job for about $1,500. I even wrote the subroutine program and tested it. All I needed was one converter box and a cable that ran between the master clock and the converter. My boss's boss completely doubted that I could do it. I did the project for $950. That saved the company $49,050. My boss wanted to give me a well-done recognition award. His boss said that he would not reward me for doing my job. I never again offered to do any task that I was not assigned to at that place.

This is a sign of an entrepreneur spirit. I knew I could do it. I was good at solving this kind of problem. It took a lot of "out of the box" thinking to propose a solution that was extremely simple and cost effective. That is what business entrepreneurs do. They see an opportunity to fill an open space in our society and they create the solution.

Entrepreneurs love being told that no matter how hard they try, they cannot succeed. Tell that to Ray Kroc and the McDonald's brother. Through their entrepreneurship they not only created a hamburger franchise worth billions of dollars, but they also created the fast food industry. How many times was Kroc told that it would never work? I don't know, but it is great that he did not listen. How many fast-food restaurants can you name?

There is a potential downside to entrepreneurial thinking. If one becomes extremely self-centered and will not listen to other people, that can lead to a mental lock, or better said, a mental prison. Even an entrepreneur must understand that he or she does not have an exclusive lock on all knowledge. Entrepreneurial spirits will sometimes believe that they have an exclusive lock on what is right and wrong.

It is the self-centered trait that will most affect how this spirit sees the biblical narratives. If the person believes that he or she has a lock on the meaning of a passage, it is difficult to break through the barrier. The sweetest thing about the Bible is that there are multiple learnings to grasp. For example, the Torah (the first five books of the Bible) are read once a year in synagogues. That means one starts with Genesis 1:1 and ends with Deuteronomy.

The Sages of Israel said that the average person will hear the Torah around seventy times in their lifetime. Therefore, there are at least seventy layers of understanding in the Torah. Each year when a narrative is read, the listener will receive a deeper message. If you are sitting in the synagogue believing that you know everything there is about the Torah, then you will not hear the deeper message that the LORD is bringing you. Here, the entrepreneurial spirit is losing out.

When dealing with this type of spirit, it is important to remember to open new avenues of thinking. Usually, the entrepreneurial spirit will see where you are going. If you can help this person to own a new way of thinking, it will open their eyes.

A biblical example is Noah. The LORD told Noah to build an Ark. His family and two of every animal, bird and insect were to join him on the Ark. The LORD made the waters of the Earth cover the planet and kill everything on land. You could have an interesting discussion with an entrepreneurial spirit about how Noah continued to do the work of the LORD while fending off the local people. This aspect is not expressed in the Genesis story. However, there had to be people mocking Noah and his sons. You could ask "What do you think Noah did when the mockers showed up?"

How about asking about why Solomon had 900+ wives? That's a lot of wives. There were cultural reasons that Solomon did this. Was this a good business move? This would make an interesting discussion.

How about touching on the edge of sacrilege? Remember that the concept of what is or not sacrilege was and is determined by the church and today is open to discussion. Is it possible that Jesus of Nazareth could have presented himself differently when he entered Jerusalem the last time? Perhaps it was not the best idea that a huge parade and fanfare occurred. Take one more step. Did such a thing happen or did an author thirty years later assume it happened? I bet I got your attention on this last question.

A Bible study leader is supposed to get the students out of their comfort zone. When they have to think about a story differently, especially one that they were told since they attended Sunday school as kids, you can get different reactions. A person who is open to different views will love the opportunity to grow. Closed- or single-minded individuals will hate you for doing it. Hey, it's a crap shoot sometimes.

If everyone in the class completely agrees with a new idea immediately, then it really was not a new idea.

Viewing the Bible as a Psychologist
(Michael H. Koplitz)

In the church, we call being a psychologist pastoral counseling. Therefore, I can write about this view of the Bible. In the United Methodist church, there are 73 distinct tasks that a pastor must perform. Yikes, how can you be good at all of them? You are right, reader; it is impossible.

Congregants may occasionally ask the pastor for professional psychological help. Whenever someone asked me for counseling, I always said "yes." Then I would consult with my wife, without mentioning names, as she has a master's degree in psychology. Sometimes I could help the person and sometimes I highly recommended that the person seek a professional.

One of things psychologists try to do is to determine what someone is thinking. They will use their body language observations, the tone of voice, and how the people construct their sentences to make a judgment. Sometimes the judgment is correct and sometimes it is not.

Often, a psychologist will brand a person as a particular personality type. I was introduced to "People Smarts" back in the early 1990s. It is a personality inventory based on psychological testing and observation. The inventory has a questionnaire with it, as all assessments do. This assessment identified personality patterns. There are four basic personality types: director (goal setter), Socializer (ego-centric), Relator (cares about others) and Thinker (analytic thinker). The last category I think should have a different name.

I learned this system and still use it. The creators gave ways to identify the primary personality type of individual. By looking at a person's work area, listening to how they talk, and seeing their actions, you can deduce the personality type. I never missed using this assessment. There is a secondary type. Therefore, everyone has a primary and a secondary type. Yes, some people can be directing directors, socializing socializers, relating relators, and thinking thinkers.

Knowing someone's personality type makes it easier to communicate. Let me give you an example. I worked with a man in the computer engineering days. Let's call him Gary. Gary learned computers on his own and joined the department. He had numerous earnings to do when it can to troubleshooting and fixing personal computers. When he got stuck, he would come to me. I was the tech guru of the department.

Let me tell you the difference between my thinking and Gary's. I am a socializing director. The primary personality type is the second one named. My primary method for solving problems was to envision the problem as a goal to be acquired. I also could think in multiple threads. I could diagnose a computer problem extremely quickly because I multi thought.

When Gary came to me, I used my multiple thinking and took him on several paths at the same time. Gary would get very frustrated and could not follow. Eventually, I gave him the answer and off he went. He got his problem solved, but he did not feel good about it. Then I learned the People Smarts personality assessment.

Gary was a thinking thinker. A trait of a thinker is that they think linearly. I needed to start with one thread of troubleshooting and work completely through it before moving to the next. It was difficult for me to work this way, but I knew if Gary was to feel good about the solution, I had to do it this way. My department relationships improved with this method of presenting information.

A psychologist understands everyone has an ego problem of one sort. A good way to view the ego is to consider it as a tool which reflects who you are. In 1995 and 1996, my bride and I taught presentation skills to a group of facilitators for a leadership program. We discussed the different attendees who were taking the classes. A person with a strong ego and is a socializer will need to answer all the questions, right or wrong. Their self-centered ego forces them to do this. They must be the center of attention, always.

How do you deal with such a student? You don't want to hurt people's feelings. However, when one person ties up the class in this manner, the other students will zone out. Sometimes it is said "Let's let someone else talk. I think Sue might have something to share." It is a slight risk that the socializer will realize they have been dominating a class. You hope the person will dial back their ego by themselves.

I attended a class on leadership for pastors. Two days before a class, a couple of people shredded me in the church at an Administrative Board meeting. The thrashing was uncalled for. This happens to pastors when they talk about the truth of the Bible, and someone does not want to hear it. I drove to the class with the instructor that day. On the way home, he told me I dominated the class. I felt bad about that. He told me that my soul was so hurt that I needed to get empathy from the group. I was allowed to dominate the discussion about my problem because the instructor knew I needed to blow off some steam.

Sometimes a person can have a strong view of the Bible from their teachings. PK (pastors' kids) can have such strong views. If their relationship was strong with their pastor parent, you could trample on their toes when you offer a different view. I had that happen once. I did not know that the person was a PK until in the Bible study group, when he yelled at me for my interpretation. Oh yes, he was a strong socializer too.

The psychologist in your Bible study will want to get into the mind of the biblical person in the narrative. Sometimes you can do it. For example, there is a lot of real estate for Abraham, Jacob, and Moses in the Bible. My definition of real estate is how many chapters of the Bible do each one of these figures received. Of course, Jesus gets the most real estate if you are a Christian because of the Christian Scriptures (New Testament).

You could create a personality index for Abraham. The psychologist in your group would love to do this. It gets dicey when there is little information in the Bible. For Jewish groups, there are plenty of other writings to examine. For Christians, there is very little behind the commentaries and they will not give you a personality assessment.

A psychologist will examine a narrative seeking human interactions. The emotions and feelings of the people will be a top priority. Understanding Jeremiah's personality can help keep the psychologist's interest in a Bible study on him. Try to tap into who the person might be.

A man named Isaiah was tapped by the LORD to become a prophet. Isaiah volunteered for the job. Who would willingly volunteer to do a job for the LORD when, in Isaiah's time, he would be killed for doing God's work? This will perk up the psychologist and keep him or her on topic with you.

Also, it will help to create a one-on-one relationship with a psychologist member of the study. It is a good idea to create good relations with everyone in your study group. Keep your eyes and ears open to learning something new!

Viewing the Bible as an Engineer
(Michael H. Koplitz)

The first 26 years of my career, I was a Computer Engineer. I say engineer because I spent a lot of time designing and implementing computer systems which entailed the hardware and software ends. In the 1970s through 1990s, there were not specialists like there are today. To do well in the field, you had to handle numerous aspects of the field. Part of that work included troubleshooting. That was one of the more difficult tasks while at my last employer. There were miles of cables, over 500 PCs and 12 mainframes, all on a shared network that had a maximum speed of 10 gb. Today's computer facilities are different and vaster than in the 1990s.

Logical thinking was a key ingredient for success in developing computer systems and networks. Another area for my success was the ability to take hardware and software and make it do things that the vendors could not image. For example, I could integrate a Burr-Brown Time and Attendance device into my DEC VAX system. Therefore, I could control the main computer from the shop floor. Both vendors said it could not be done and I like that kind of challenge.

The ability to create seamless computer systems was paramount. An engineer must understand the system that he or she is about to work on or create. That includes the mechanical and electrical specifications. Also, abstract thinking is important. As an engineer, visualize the finished product so that you can create a goal to accomplish. You do not have to visualize the final GUI (Graphics User Interface), you have to know the information that will be displayed.

Engineers like facts. I can say that after college, I read one fictional book. Reading fiction does not help me improve my engineering skills required for the job, but not all engineers dislike reading fiction. The uninformed person will see a lot of fiction in the Bible. Therefore, the Bible is not viewed as a book that should be sacred.

The Bible is not a book of fiction. It is a Semitic book that was written totally differently than Greek oriented books. The Bible is filled with metaphors and similes and other such language mechanisms. If a true engineer wanted to get past the fiction view, then he or she would search out the Near East interpretation.

A man named Noah was commanded by the LORD to build an Ark. Noah had no skill in building a boat, especially one the size the LORD commanded him to build. Imagine what Noah's wife said when Noah told her. "Are you nuts.?We live hundreds of leagues from the sea." You can envision the argument they had.

Was there a huge flood or one that flooded the area in which civilization was planted? Today we call that area Iraq and Iran. In ancient times, it was called Mesopotamia. It is not the actual story that matters. It is the lesson from the story that is important. Semitic story tellers love to embellish stories. The more embellishment, the better. It is not the actual story that matters, but the lesson from the story.

Engineers will have trouble understanding this concept because they use precise language, and the Bible does not in most stories. It should be noted that for a Semitic writer, the Bible is precise. For the Engineer, it is not. Therefore, the stories of the Bible will have to be interpreted in a logical and precise manner for the Engineer.

The bottom line for this type of person is that an Engineer is trained deeply in western method. They seek facts and formulas. The Bible is a Near Eastern book filled with analogies and metaphors. Therefore, thinking in facts and formulas can be difficult to view analogies as not being facts. Numbers in the Bible may not be factual but metaphors. For example, the number 40 in the Bible shows the completion of a purpose. Jesus was in the desert for 40 days. The 40 shows that God's task for him, to prepare him for his ministry, was complete. It does not mean he spent 40 full days in the desert. He might have spent that much time but that is not what the Bible is concerned about. This is a difficult understanding for those of us who were taught by western teaching methods.

Viewing the Bible as a Leader
(Michael H. Koplitz)

Over the past decades, people have defined many leadership styles. I use the Blake and Mouton Leadership grid when discussing leadership. In this model, there are nine different leadership styles. A problem with defining how a leader will view the Bible is that most authors will lump all nine styles into one and call it "leadership." My paper on the Leadership Grid was over 60 pages long. Therefore, I will summarize each style. There are several sources available that describe all the details of the Leadership grid.

There are some leadership principles that apply to all nine leadership styles. A leader seeks the truth, the accuracy of a situation, and develops a direction for the team. However, as you will see, some of the leadership styles are not as demanding in some areas.

Seven styles: do nothing, relationship, goal, middle, opportunist, paternalist, team leader. Let me offer a couple of things here. The basic premise for the leadership grid is that it is a comparison of how the leader weighs relationship building versus goal accomplishment.

In 2006-2007, I sent the Blake and Mouton leadership grid assessment to seventy pastors in my district of the United Methodist Church. Enough responded to get an accurate assessment. The results are available if you wish to view them.

Let's start with the "do nothing" leader. My 25 years of experience taught me that this is the optimal style in most churches. Why? The members of the congregation usually want the church to behave in a defined way. When a new pastor arrives at a church and tries to change things, the people usually revolt. The "do nothing" leadership style does not mean that the leader is not concerned about goals and relationships. It means that the leader will walk on the outside of decisions, especially the major ones. The leader will only offer information and direction if directly asked. It is safe simply to be the support of anything, well, except something non-biblical. The bullets and arrows that people in the church like to throw will not be at the pastor. OK, that is an inaccurate statement because sometimes opposing sides will try to force the pastor to pick a side. The "do nothing" leadership style will only become a problem when this happens. In the UMC system, this leadership style pastor will request a move if there is any sign that this situation might happen. In a biblical study, this leadership style will sit back and let people say and believe whatever they want. The pastor with this leadership style will allow any interpretations that might be offered in the class to go unchallenged. This leader thinks that if they offer anything, it will offend someone, and they cannot allow it. It is better to allow inaccurate and non-biblical interpretations because it will avoid all problems. So, this leadership style will view the Bible in any way the congregation wants with no challenge. No teaching or expansion of understanding will happen with this pastor.

The "relationship over goals" leader will view a Bible study as being an opportunity to make friends and strengthen relationships. This leader will halt a conflict over interpreting a passage in the Bible. Instead of a discussion that could lead to conflict with this, the leader will stop the class and hold a hug session. Relationships are more important than accuracy in this leadership style. Therefore, the people in the congregation will love one another but will not advance in their biblical understanding. If the leader is a pastor, the sermons will be a conglomeration of stories that may or may not relate to the read biblical passage. After all, it is not the learning that is as important as everyone loving each other.

The "goals over relationships" leader will be the opposite of the one just described. This leader wants to accomplish goals. The leader will set before a Bible study class the goals to be achieved. The concern for the relationships between the members of the class is important if they do not interfere with obtaining the goals. If the leader determines several sessions are to devote to a study, you can be guaranteed that it will be done in the defined time frame. It does not matter if the attendees fully understand the study. The goal is to be done by a deadline. Oh yes, that deadline is self-imposed, well, usually. The warm fuzzy feeling may not be there.

The "middle of the road" leader weighs relationships and goals at the same time. It is important to accomplish goals but also relationships must be built. This leadership style will use any defined rule book as the guide. Therefore, if the pastor says to this leader, get the study done in ten weeks, the leader is thrilled. The responsibility of getting the job done within a time frame is not their decision. This leader loves it when given directions from a superior. It is easy to said, "the pastor gave me ten weeks to get this done." If there is an objection, then this leadership style leader will point to the superior as the problem. From a pastor's point of view, he/she will look to the church's governing body to tell him/her what to do.

The "opportunist" leadership style is when a leader uses any of the six leadership styles, depending on the situation. Usually, this style causes people to not trust the leader. The example is when saying one thing to a person and then the complete opposite to another. People understand when this happens. The view of the Bible and its interpretation depends on who is the leader speaking with. This leader can determine what must be said to make the leader look good. Therefore, the accuracy of interpretation will suffer. The leader will provide multiple interpretations which may not link, resulting in confusion.

The "paternalist" is a leadership style who expects the followers to "come under his/her wing." This style should be called the "paternalistic/maternalistic" style. This leader will expect the participants to follow his/her lead. Whatever this leader says about interpreting the Bible is all that counts and as a participant, you had better like it. If a student creates too numerous difficulties for the leader, that student will be asked to leave the study. It is harsh when it happens. Remember that this leadership style believes that he/she knows everything, and you better agree. Sounds a lot like college professors. Did I say that out loud? Oops.

The "team leader" leadership style is the most effective. This leader knows how to accomplish goals while making the participants happy. Relationship building is as important as accomplishing goals. Studies that are run by this leadership style are usually happy to get together and learn together. The leader listens to and acknowledges everyone's contributions in the group. This leadership style is usually open to various thoughts and will encourage debate. However, this leader knows how to stop a debate from turning ugly.

I am going to give an example that some readers will consider heresy. My apologies up front to anyone who might feel offended by such a thought. Ok, here it is. How would the different leadership styles handle the question: Does it matter if Mary, Jesus' mother, was a virgin? I bet some readers just got angry. I once asked that question and a participant of the class wanted to punch me in the face for saying such a thing. I did not say that Mary was not a virgin. I asked a question. Remember that the question is not if Mary was a virgin. The question is, does it matter either way? Would your faith in Jesus change if Mary was not a virgin?

The first thing to consider is what does each of the different leadership style leaders think about that question? For example, if the paternalist said, "absolutely," then the discussion will be pushed in that direction. Of course, if the paternalist does not believe in a virgin birth, the leader will defend the position with a lot of force. The free exchange of ideas probably will not occur.

The "do nothing" leader will sit back and let things fly. This leader will avoid any obstacle thrown their way. It will not matter what the leader's position is on the subject. The leader will let the group work on the question until they arrive at some conclusion. This is a question that this leader will want to avoid. Conflict is bad, from this leader's point of view. All conflict does is cause relationships to break and may not allow the accomplishment of a goal. However, the leader ducking all discussions allows the leader to be safe and secure.

The "goal over relationships" leader will strive to get a consensus, or at least most of the attendees, to agreed to a solution to the question. A potential problem here is that the leader's belief will come through and be a part of any discussion. If the leader develops a goal in their head that their belief must win the day, he/she will push the agenda. The problem is not solved until the people come to an understanding at least equivalent to the leader.

The "relationship over goals" leaders will fear this type of discussion. The leader would fear that the discussion will lead to conflict that could break relationships. The discussion would be brief. There will not be a clear direction or decision. The leader will quickly want to change the subject. It does not matter what side of the question this leader takes. The leader will consider this as a threat to the relationship and will avoid it at any cost, except for the relationships. That's the purchase of a Bible study group to this leader style.

The "paternalistic/maternalistic" style will push his/her idea. It does not matter what the leader believes. The paternalistic/maternalistic style will push their idea relentlessly, regardless of the leader's beliefs.

The "opportunist" leader will simply agreed with everyone and will not take a formal position. The same will occur with the "middle of the road" leader. If there is a rule book, like a church doctrine, this leadership style will grab it and use it. Therefore, the leader is not hurt.

I have identified the seven leadership types and how they would react to people in a Bible study. How a Bible study leader deals with the people in the group will determine its success or failure. If you can understand what viewpoint a person has the easier it will be to connect with the person. Your leadership style will determine how you lead a Bible study.

Learn what your leadership style and the benefits and the warning when running a study group. It will help you in your communication methods.

Viewing the Bible as a Scientist
(Michael H. Koplitz)

When I worked at Warner-Lambert Co. in Lititz, PA, my boss was a Ph.D., an Automated Chemist. One day I said to him I was a computer engineer because I was building the network and creating systems for the manufacturing floor. He clarified I was a scientist. There are apparent differences between the two careers. In my case, I was performing both career options at the same time. To fix a networking problem, you need to guess what might be wrong before trying to solve it. When the boss clearly says you are a scientist, you are a scientist.

The first thing a scientist does is to create a hypothesis of results. Scientists test hypotheses to confirm or reject them. If the hypothesis is wrong, the scientist will create a new one using the test results and assumptions from the previous one.

Scientists seek the truth of a situation. However, the laws of physics and nature will plague the scientist who are seeking concrete data. For example, how could God create the Universe in seven days? A day is only twenty-four hours long. To answer this question, one has to dig into the Kabbalah. It was Kabbalistic rabbis in the 16th century who determined how long a "God Day" was. They offered the age of the Universe, not in thousands but in billions of years. Those first Kabbalistic rabbis were close to the number of years that science offers today.

A scientist would approach the Bible seeking facts, not fiction. Their analytic way of deducing answers would get in the way because the Bible was not written in that manner. First, the culture of the day is missing. If you wrote in your diary that you went to the grocery store today, which was 9 miles away, you would not have to write that you owned a car. Perhaps you borrowed a car, but today we don't include our culture in our writings unless it is imperative. The same thing applied to the biblical authors. They did not have to describe every aspect of their culture. After all, everyone on that day knew their culture. Do you know how ancient Israelites, or even the first Christians, lived? It is known that the first Jewish followers of Christ still went to the Temple in Jerusalem to offer sacrifices for the forgiveness of sin.

A scientist would have been trained in the classical Greek method. When someone is taught in the classical Greek method, it's difficult to open their mind. The Greek method of learning, which we in the west have learned, is restrictive. It says that the teacher is the expert and to not question their authority or knowledge. That's it in a summary. The authors of the Bible were Semitic people who wrote completely differently.

The Bible is filled with metaphors, analogies, hyperbole, and the Semitic way of writing. The scientist will use their Greek style learning to understand a Semitic document. It does not work well. However, the scientist will be happy to read the biblical narrative word for word and interpret it that way. They do not know how else to do it.

Therefore, a story like David and Goliath cannot be true because a boy could not throw a small rock that would land between the giant's eyes. There was a small part of the nose and forehead that was not covered. Even if it did, it would not have killed him. To the scientist, this story cannot be true. If a story is not true, how much of the Bible can be trusted as factual?

Note that I used the word factual. When a theologian is writing a book, it is based heavily on faith. When a scientist reads that book, they seek any facts that the author wrote. The determination of the validity of the story is based on facts, culture, situation, and faith.

Did Sarah have a child when she was close to one hundred years old? That is biologically impossible. I believed that there was something wrong with this story. My biology training told me so. However, over time, my spiritual soul came forward and I accept Sarah being 90+ years old when Isaac was born. It is not Sarah's age that is important. It is important that she prayed to the LORD to grant this one special gift. The LORD gave Sarah the gift because of her prayers. The scientist wants a logical explanation. Sometimes if take faith that the story is authentic. Using the concept of metaphors and analogies with hyperbole can baffle the Scientist.

The pastor and biblical class leader will need to help the scientist get over reading the Bible literally. A problem in church is that many people have been told that someone must read the Bible literally. A cultural problem that arises from reading the Bible literally is a section of the book of Daniel. The Emperor of Persia runs out of his palace and eats grass. After which the Bible says that he was eaten by worms. This section must not be read literally. Why? Because if you did, you got the entire story wrong.

The emperor eating grass is a metaphor, meaning that he was going mad. The emperor was losing his mind. Today we call it dementia. He did not go to the yard and eat grass with the cows. Being eaten by worms may occur in the grave but when used to discuss the living it means that the emperor had cancer. The medicines of biblical times were not good. Numerous things were not discovered until now. When a person died of cancer and they cut the body open, like an autopsy, the organs would appear to have been eaten. Cancers feed off the healthy cells of the body. To the ancients, it appeared as if worms ate him from the inside. Thus, the metaphor was created.

The pastor and Bible study leader must help the scientist let go of facts and figures and concentrate on the abstract message of the Bible. That will be a difficult job for the scientist to accomplish. There are plenty of examples in the Bible that you can use.

Another example is Jonah in the big fish story. Yes, it was a big fish, not a whale. How can a person live in the stomach of a big fish for three days? No, you cannot. However, numbers in the Bible are used to represent ideas. The number three is a sacred number which always refers to the LORD.

It is not the physical three days that are important but that Jonah called upon the three, that is the LORD to save him. Jonah ran away from God after being told to visit Nineveh because God intended to save them. Running away was a sign of disloyalty or disbelief in God. So, God followed Jonah and had the big fish swallow him so that Jonah would understand that God lived outside the land of Israel and could find him anywhere on Earth. The number three automatically tells the reader that God was about to do something.

Once being a scientist, I could change my thinking from pure facts to a faith in the words of the Bible. The new view was through the way Semitic people wrote, their culture, and faith in God that there are messages in the Bible that He wants us to discover. Understanding that God's Word has many interpretations helped me transform.

Viewing the Bible as a Pastor
(Robert Cook & Michael Koplitz

Robert's view:

As we come to this final chapter, together we have already explored how the Bible can be interpreted by those in a variety of disciplines and vocations. But in this chapter, we will explore how a theologically trained pastor will seek to interpret a biblical text.

As noted previously, one's social location pre-fits a set of lenses by which one may interpret a biblical text. The pastor's task is to be aware of what lenses by which they approach a text and decide how useful or not such lenses may be.

The pastor's social location along with their theological orientation typically predetermine the outcome. But often, this is not *exegesis*—drawing out from a text what is there and its context; but *eisegesis*, or leading our own ideas into a text. Being aware of these distinctions, regardless of social or theological orientation, is important to get at the original meaning of the text.

The typical seminary trained pastor has taken classes on biblical interpretation using the rules of hermeneutics, from the Greek word *hermeneuo,* which applies a series of rules of interpretation and application of biblical texts. Hermeneutical rules provide a way of integrity to the understanding and interpretation of a text. Biblical interpretation is more than knowing a set of rules, but it cannot be done without the rules. So, learning the rules, and rightly applying them is foundational to rightly understand scripture.

There are many hermeneutical rules, but all begin understanding that one must take scripture seriously. While some texts are literal, such as "Thou Shall Not Kill", while others are metaphoric or allegoric, as with

Jonah being swallowed by a whale. The first rule is that scripture interprets scripture. There is an interconnection between all of the biblical canon. One should avoid building an interpretation on just a single verse. Rather one needs to use a concordance to review passages that have a relationship to the passage you seek to understand.

Secondly, the meaning of a word, a phrase or paragraph must be derived from its context. One cannot reduce a text to just a "sound byte," as is commonly done with contemporary speeches or memes. No one passage can be divorced from the surrounding verses or from the whole of scripture. The interpreter will find cultural, cultic, and linguistic threads that they will need to research. Fortunately, the average interpreter has access to in-print and online helps that can be used to further their understanding. This may not be a quick and easy process, although oftentimes it can be. Biblical interpretation with integrity can be demanding, but very rewarding and worth the effort one must put in to it.

A third rule in hermeneutics is that the goal in interpretation is to discover what God desires to be known and understood, rather than seeking to derive your own unique interpretation of some hidden truth. Biblical interpretation is not a tarot reading or the uncovering of some dark mystery. It is to bring to light God's revelation.

There have been many religious movements and cults down through the ages that offer "deep" or "unique" interpretations of the Bible. Those who have come up with "deep and unique" interpretations are usually wrong. With two millennia of biblical scholarship, there is a solid tradition of biblical interpretation that is consistent across many theological traditions. And if an interpretation of a text is inconsistent with the tradition of scholarship, it is likely saying things the original authors never intended.

A fourth rule is to *not* interpret a biblical text in light of one's personal experience but interpret it in light of scripture. One's personal experience is already colored by their social status, gender, theological training and tradition and also by their peer group. These lenses can be useful in one's self-understanding, but not as a means of understanding what a biblical text is saying. If one insists on an interpretation based upon personal experience, essentially, they are saying because they have had a particular experience, this must also be true of scripture. This is simply not a reliable way to interpret a biblical text, or for that matter the Bible itself.

A fifth rule and a most vital rule is that the original meaning of a text must be understood in its original language. Most people do not study biblical Hebrew,

Aramaic or Greek. And while there is now a plethora of translations of the Bible in English, they may not exactly get the sense intended by the original author.

However, there are many helpful resources that will guide the interpreter to a better understanding of the original language of the passage in which it was first written. Many concordances have Hebrew and Greek lexicons. Commentaries also will help you to discover the sense originally intended by an author. There are also many volumes by Jewish and Christian authors which offer good and reliable interpretations of a passage.

A sixth rule is to understand the historical background of a text. One must research and explore the background of the times and social location in which a book or passage of scripture came about. There will always be a spiritual principle that is timeless, but it cannot be properly understood apart from the knowledge of its cultural and historical background.

An example of this is found in Romans 12:19: **"If your enemy is hungry, feed him; If he is thirsty, give him a drink; For in so doing you will heap coals of fire on his head." (NLV.)** This sounds off-putting to the contemporary reader. But the historic context demonstrates the actual kindness and paradoxic quality of what was a common metaphor in St. Paul's time.

The poorest people, often widows, needed a way to generate income. One way was to provide live coals by which others could quickly start their fires in the morning. One would arise very early and build a good size fire. As the fuel burned down to coals, they would place the hot coal on an earthen platter and then walk through their neighborhood selling the live coals to those seeking to more quickly get their fires going for cooking or for warmth. This provided the seller with warmth as well an income.

Another example is found in Matthew 5:13 ***"You are the salt of the earth. But what good is salt if it has lost its flavor? Can you make it salty again? It will be thrown out and trampled underfoot as worthless."*** So, in the day, how was table salt obtained? The easiest place was at the Dead Sea area. A layer of soil covered the ground but underneath was a layer of salt. One put their shovel into the ground and turned up a clod of salt. Turned upside down, they gathered the salt as needed until their got down to the soil. Then it was thrown out. Knowing that illumines the text and provides insight to the context Jesus used. So, understanding the historical and social context is essential to an accurate interpretation.

A seventh rule is that of the unity of the scriptures as a whole. That is, that parts of scripture must be understood in relationship to the whole of scripture. Therefore, an interpretation must have coherence with the rest of scripture.

The editors of the Hebrew scriptures, writing in the times during and after the Babylonian Captivity (C. 586-515 BCE), intended for their scrolls of history, prophetic writings and poetry to tell the story of the Hebrew people so their descendants would understand who they were in relation to the covenant God made with Abraham, many centuries before. But the writings made clear that they were a part of something greater than they at first understood. What was emerging was a world class religion based upon the actions of God among their people. They discovered a unity in their writings that was greater than they knew. The early compilers of the New Testament used the rule of unity as they gathered and edited various writings of the New Testament period. Writings inconsistent, such as the Gospel of Thomas or the Gospel of Jude, were rejected from the canon of scripture because they were inconsistent with the unity of scripture.

The pastor also must bear in mind that types are symbolic of reality. In the ancient Hebrew cultus, symbolism and types characterize the Tabernacle and subsequently, the temple. St. Paul speaks of both Adam and Jesus as types of humanity. Investigating the background and placement in scripture of types and symbols requires care and good scholarship. Is a type representing an action—such as Moses lifting up the bronze serpent; or an office—as with the priesthood: an event- such as the wandering in the wilderness of the children of Israel; or an experience, such as entering the tabernacle or the temple? All of these have polyvalent meanings and getting at them responsibly and accurately is the pastor's task.

One can research other hermeneutical rules for biblical interpretation and they are essential so that one does not transpose their own opinion, context or belief onto a text or to the whole of scripture. To do so is irresponsible. So, pastors do have to learn and understand these rules as principles to reading and rightly interpreting scripture.

Interpreting scripture is also contextual. History shows that very often scripture has been taken out of context and used to prop up a doctrine or belief that it does not actually support. In 19th century America such misunderstandings appear to be prolific, though most of those interpretations faded quickly. In order to interpret scripture contextually, the pastor needs to understand whether a particular text was meant as a metaphor, an allegory, as a prophetic exhortation or as history before seeking to apply it to their own time and setting. While one may try to use scripture to fit their purposes and to say what they want, a right interpretation tends to mitigate against such misuses.

While pastors have filters based on their education and experience. It is difficult to learn about the Bible because it's difficult to see through these filters. It is a good thing to listen closely to a sermon and even fact check it. Personally, I welcome challenges to a sermon. I think that being open to hear from one who has listened carefully and offers a critique or a challenge is incumbent upon one who will preach Scripture as the Word of God. The scriptures are, after all, a dialogue with God about the human condition. Through dialogue we drop our defensiveness and become open to one another and find new ways to understand our faith.

Michael's view

I did not grow up in the church, therefore I do not have a set of paradigms about what church and the Bible are about. When I came to know Jesus Christ, I wanted to learn everything I could. I aim to study the Bible's original meaning, especially Jesus' words, and share my findings with everyone as part of my calling from Christ. That has been a 25-plus year adventure.

Let me say that there are four major categories of pastors. Yes, I am generalizing a bit, so please do not get offended if you feel you are. We all have a piece of each type in us. There are the conservatives, liberal, progressive, and research pastors. How can I make this observation? Before I make this observation, I would like to mention that the way the Bible is perceived can be influenced by the denomination the pastor grew up in.

I should mention that a new group of pastors is emerging. They are the progressive pastors. They like to say that the Bible is a group of ancient stories that do not apply to us today. Therefore, since they discount the

Bible, anything goes. That is how they justify accepting whatever our society determines is acceptable. They are concerned with society's acceptance of them before biblical acceptance.

One last type of pastor which is the category I fit into. That type is the biblical researcher. In order to fulfill Jesus' call, I became a biblical researcher. I offer the original meaning of the Bible in my sermons. Yes, there are areas I do not offer original meaning in the church because it may be contrary to what people have heard for years.

The conservative pastor will view the Bible literally. The conservative pastor will believe that there are no errors in the Bible. Even if there appears to be an error, he will not accept it. According to the conservative pastor, the stories in the Bible must be viewed as completely real and should not be interpreted differently. Christian

Fundamentalista are a good example of this thinking. A little boy named David killed a giant named Goliath with one stone.

The liberal pastor will view the David and Goliath story as a pleasant story that really did not happen. This pastor will insist that the story is about having faith in God no matter what the situation or difficulties are. That is a good interpretation of the allegorical meaning of the story, however the historical account is completely ignored.

The progressive pastor will not discuss the story unless it can fit it into whatever lesson is to be learned. The pastor could recognize that Israel briefly oppressed the Philistines and that David's success made it right.

As a biblical researcher, I understand Semitic people wrote the Bible. Semitic writers wrote completely differently than their Greek and Western counterparts. Hence, we must interpret the David and Goliath story as a metaphor, since it was written by Semitic people who had a unique writing style than their Greek and Western counterparts. Every aspect of the story tells the tale of faith in the LORD.

Adding Personality Types into the Mix
(Michael H. Koplitz)

A note about Adams' "Loserthink" book is that he does not consider people's personality types. I will admit up front that this is going to be extremely difficult to almost impossible to do. Such a synthesis would be extremely long, thus putting you to the reader into a reading coma. Therefore, it is not prudent to do that because how can you recommend this book to friends and family if you are in a coma? Lol.

Every type of career mentioned in this book has generalizations about how the person would use their career training niche to view the Bible. However, there are other factors that led to a person's view of the Bible and actually everything in life. I learned that when I worked in the computing field in my first career. Personality types are important to understand.

Some of you probably heard about the Myers-Brigg personality assessment. This was the flagship during the end of the last century. I took the assessment several times in many leadership training courses. I always came out as INTJ (introvert, intuitive, thinker, judger). The problem with this approach is that there are sixteen different types. I cannot remember sixteen different types. Also, the analysis of the Myers-Brigg is not useful unless you can get colleagues or family members to do the assessment.

In the mid-1990s I discovered "People Smarts." The creators offered tangible ways to assess a person's core personality by paying attention to their conversation, office, and clothing. There are four personality types and each of the four has a secondary type, which is one of the four. Yes, that gives you sixteen types, but they are easy to remember because you only have to memorize four types.

There are the Socializers, Directors, Relators, and the Analytics (the instrument calls this group the Thinkers but I think that is misleading). The Socializers have ego-centric personalities. The Directors are goal-oriented people. The Relators are people oriented. Analytics are linear thinkers. Each of the four areas I described is the primary type. Each primary type has a second type. Therefore, one could be a Socializing Director (the first one is the secondary trait, the second one is the primary trait), for example. The attributes of an ego-centric personality who likes to get goals accomplished.

Let me give you some of the office type examples. If I walked into an office and saw pictures of the person's family surrounding their work area, I am probably dealing with a Relator. If the person has their degrees and accomplishments behind them on a wall for all to see when speaking to him/her, the person is probably a Socializer.

A Director's desk is usually messy looking because they are goal setters who can perform multiple tasks. Every pile of paper is another project. The Director knows what each pile is about. The Analytic person has a clean desk and places one task on the desk at a time. Before they go home for the day, everything is returned to its proper file folder in the filing cabinet.

I described the leadership grid in the Leader article, and you can see how it connects to the People Smarts grid. I can honestly say I have never missed the boat in determining a person's personality type. The secondary type can get tricky. I have had people take the assessment and get upset because they discover that their second trait is not what they expected.

I gave the assessment out to the pastors of the York District of the Central PA Conference of the United Methodist church. I was shocked by the results. My hypothesis was that an overwhelming number of pastors would be Relators. Now for the shocker…over 75% were Socializers.

I thought that could not be correct. I checked the results three times and got the same result. Socializers. Then I did some interviews and found over 75% of the pastors I interviewed said that the best church experience was when the church did things his/her way. A pastor is the center of attention on Sunday. Right? Therefore, it is not surprising to see these results.

The Bishops in the UMC make decisions that benefit them and not the people sitting in the pews. Of course, 75% of them are Socializers. Ego-centric people make decisions that are beneficial to them! That is a reason the UMC is failing. But let me not get off on a tangent.

The person's career will give them the tools to view the Bible in a certain way. I consider that the macro-vision of interpreting the narratives. The micro-vision is their personality type. For the teacher or pastor, understanding the personality types of the students can allow for the presentation of information that will be most effective. Pastors and teachers should present information in multiple ways to fit different views of the Bible. By presenting information in a way that each personality type can connect with will help in the understanding of the Bible.

The book cannot accommodate connecting the sixteen personality types in the People Smarts assessment with all the careers. In the same way, it is not possible to examine every career to see how a person will relate to the biblical narrative.

Conclusion
(Michael H. Koplitz)

If this material is more complex than we have shown you, why present the material at all? It is to get you to understand how to use the person's career and personality type to get a message across. The best pastors and teachers learn how to do that. The first step is to make you aware of how people will view the same narratives in different ways.

We hope you will do some of your own research and learn about this topic. Take it to the next level. Learn about the Leadership Grid and the People Smarts assessment. You will discover how you will relate to people at a deeper level, especially if you use the People Smarts method.

Always remember that there are numerous levels to God's Word. The rabbis say that there are at least seventy layers in the Torah. I think that there are a lot more. Rabbi Steinsaltz said that every person can develop their own Torah because of their personal understanding of the Word. No one's interpretation is better or worse than another person's.

If we have accomplished anything for you, we hope that is the point. Respect everyone's opinion and interpretation as long as it is biblical. Viewing the Bible differently is God's gift to us. No right, no wrong, all God!

God bless you for deciding to read our book. We pray that you have been blessed by its contents and will search for more.

You can find all of Michael's work at http://michaelkoplitz.info and on Amazon.

May the blessings of the LORD be upon you and your family always. Amen.

Biographies

Michael Harvey Koplitz, D.Min, Ph.D.

Michael H. Koplitz was an ordained church pastor for 25 years and now is a full-time biblical researcher. He has a Bachelor's of Science degree in Biology and Computer Science from Dickinson College, Carlisle, PA; a Master of Divinity degree from Lancaster Theological Seminary which is now a part of Moravian University, Lancaster, PA; a Doctorate in Ministry in Christian Leadership from Gordon-Conwell Theological Seminary, Charlotte, NC; is a Ph.D. from The Bible Learning University, Albuquerque, NM. He is an ordained Messianic Jewish Rabbi. He was authored over 1000 research papers on biblical passages and several commentaries on biblical books. You can find his work at *http://michaelkoplitz.info.*

Sandra Jean Koplitz, MS.

Sandra has been a teacher in Middle and High School for thirty years. She has been involved in several areas of education besides teaching her favorite subject, which is Spanish. She has been a devoted and dedicated teacher who always put her students first. She attended Dickinson College, Carlisle, PA and earned her Bachelor of Arts degree. She earned a Master's of Science degree in Psychology from Shippensburg University, Shippensburg, PA.

Sandra earned her Local Pastor's license in the United Methodist church and had an integral part in Michael's ministry work for 25 years. Currently, she works with Michael on several biblical research projects.

Deborah Hill, LCSW

Deborah Hill is a retired clinical social worker with over thirty years' experience in public and private service. She has a Master's degree in Clinical Social Work and a Bachelor's in Anthropology and Photography.

She developed lectures and multi-media presentations for universities, public schools, foster care agencies and volunteer organizations, teaching how to heal from stress, burnout, trauma, and relationship issues.

She has authored several clinical books including <u>Open, the Therapist is in, 101 Mental Health and Wellness Counseling Insights book and workbook,</u> <u>When a Loved One is Traumatized,</u> and <u>Creating Healthy Relationships.</u>

She has written two fiction novels, <u>Death in Disguise</u> and <u>The Revelation</u> under the name Deborah Sickle

Hill. She is currently working on a four-book saga and enjoys time with her grandchildren.

A. Robert Cook, D.Min

Rev. Dr Robert Cook is an ordained Elder in the United Methodist Church, currently serving as a Teaching Elder in the Presbyterian Church USA (Greencastle Presbyterian Church, Greencastle, PA). He holds degrees from the University of Valley Forge, Drew University, Johns-Hopkins University and the Pittsburgh Theological Seminary. Rev. Dr. Cook has been a career pastor serving a variety of congregations since 1979. His interest in biblical scholarship has led him to guide congregations to a deeper understanding of scripture and in the practice of faith.

* 9 7 9 8 2 2 7 8 5 8 7 7 1 *